What am I reading?
Log Book and Journal

This book belongs to:

....

If found, please contact me at:

....

How do you use this journal?

The short answer is, of course, however you want. If you looked at some of the pages and wondered what I meant for you to do with them, though, here's your answer.

Let me walk you through the journal.

1) Instruction Page
   This is where you are right now. Ta-da!

2) Quick Tracker Pages
   Did you reread a book? Was it a quick read you don't feel like taking the time to document? Log it here so you have a record without all the work. (Space for 30 books.)

3) Book List
   Think of this as a table of contents. The numbers of the lines correspond to the page numbers of the log pages. Add the book, author, and star rating next to the log page number so you'll be able to find it later.

4) Book Logs
   Keep track of everything about the books from your book list here. This journal has space for 120 logs.

5)Favorites (Reads, Quotes, Characters, and more)
   Make a list of those truly special books, impactful quotes, loveable characters, and more. The fourth favorites section has been left blank for you to decide which of your favorite items to gather together.

5) Customizable Trackers
   Sometimes there's things we want to track about our books. Whether it's how much of a particular genre we're reading, what type of authors we're choosing, how many volumes we're buying or borrowing from the library, or something else.   More>>>

5) Customizable Trackers Continued
   To use these trackers, list your defining characteristics in the key and give each one a color. For each book you read, color in one section of the tracker with the appropriate color.
   Some data sets to consider:
   Genre: Contemporary romance, Historical romance, Mystery, theology, self-help, etc.
   Procurement: Bought, Already owned, public library, library app, borrowed from friend, etc.
   Format: Paperback, hardback, ebook, audio
   Anything else you want to see patterns on.

6) Reading Goal Trackers
   Got a reading goal to track? Take care of it here! There's room for three custom goals and a year long tracker so you can log which days you read

7) TBR Lists
   Want to keep track of other books you want to read? Don't want to forget the rest of a series or an author's back list? These pages are the perfect place to list books you want to read in the future, ARCs you've signed up to review, or those impulse buys you want to keep track of.

Quick Tracker

Book Name	Author	Date Finished	Rating
			☆☆☆☆☆
			☆☆☆☆☆
			☆☆☆☆☆
			☆☆☆☆☆
			☆☆☆☆☆
			☆☆☆☆☆
			☆☆☆☆☆
			☆☆☆☆☆
			☆☆☆☆☆
			☆☆☆☆☆
			☆☆☆☆☆
			☆☆☆☆☆
			☆☆☆☆☆
			☆☆☆☆☆
			☆☆☆☆☆

Quick Tracker

Book Name	Author	Date Finished	Rating
			☆☆☆☆☆
			☆☆☆☆☆
			☆☆☆☆☆
			☆☆☆☆☆
			☆☆☆☆☆
			☆☆☆☆☆
			☆☆☆☆☆
			☆☆☆☆☆
			☆☆☆☆☆
			☆☆☆☆☆
			☆☆☆☆☆
			☆☆☆☆☆
			☆☆☆☆☆
			☆☆☆☆☆
			☆☆☆☆☆

Book List

pg	Book Name	Author	Rating
13			☆☆☆☆☆
14			☆☆☆☆☆
15			☆☆☆☆☆
16			☆☆☆☆☆
17			☆☆☆☆☆
18			☆☆☆☆☆
19			☆☆☆☆☆
20			☆☆☆☆☆
21			☆☆☆☆☆
22			☆☆☆☆☆
23			☆☆☆☆☆
24			☆☆☆☆☆
25			☆☆☆☆☆
26			☆☆☆☆☆
27			☆☆☆☆☆
28			☆☆☆☆☆
29			☆☆☆☆☆
30			☆☆☆☆☆
31			☆☆☆☆☆
32			☆☆☆☆☆

Book List

pg	Book Name	Author	Rating
33			☆☆☆☆☆
34			☆☆☆☆☆
35			☆☆☆☆☆
36			☆☆☆☆☆
37			☆☆☆☆☆
38			☆☆☆☆☆
39			☆☆☆☆☆
40			☆☆☆☆☆
41			☆☆☆☆☆
42			☆☆☆☆☆
43			☆☆☆☆☆
44			☆☆☆☆☆
45			☆☆☆☆☆
46			☆☆☆☆☆
47			☆☆☆☆☆
48			☆☆☆☆☆
49			☆☆☆☆☆
50			☆☆☆☆☆
51			☆☆☆☆☆
52			☆☆☆☆☆

Book List

pg	Book Name	Author	Rating
53			☆☆☆☆☆
54			☆☆☆☆☆
55			☆☆☆☆☆
56			☆☆☆☆☆
57			☆☆☆☆☆
58			☆☆☆☆☆
59			☆☆☆☆☆
60			☆☆☆☆☆
61			☆☆☆☆☆
62			☆☆☆☆☆
63			☆☆☆☆☆
64			☆☆☆☆☆
65			☆☆☆☆☆
66			☆☆☆☆☆
67			☆☆☆☆☆
68			☆☆☆☆☆
69			☆☆☆☆☆
70			☆☆☆☆☆
71			☆☆☆☆☆
72			☆☆☆☆☆

Book List

pg	Book Name	Author	Rating
73			☆☆☆☆☆
74			☆☆☆☆☆
75			☆☆☆☆☆
76			☆☆☆☆☆
77			☆☆☆☆☆
78			☆☆☆☆☆
79			☆☆☆☆☆
80			☆☆☆☆☆
81			☆☆☆☆☆
82			☆☆☆☆☆
83			☆☆☆☆☆
84			☆☆☆☆☆
85			☆☆☆☆☆
86			☆☆☆☆☆
87			☆☆☆☆☆
88			☆☆☆☆☆
89			☆☆☆☆☆
90			☆☆☆☆☆
91			☆☆☆☆☆
92			☆☆☆☆☆

Book List

pg	Book Name	Author	Rating
93			☆☆☆☆☆
94			☆☆☆☆☆
95			☆☆☆☆☆
96			☆☆☆☆☆
97			☆☆☆☆☆
98			☆☆☆☆☆
99			☆☆☆☆☆
100			☆☆☆☆☆
101			☆☆☆☆☆
102			☆☆☆☆☆
103			☆☆☆☆☆
104			☆☆☆☆☆
105			☆☆☆☆☆
106			☆☆☆☆☆
107			☆☆☆☆☆
108			☆☆☆☆☆
109			☆☆☆☆☆
110			☆☆☆☆☆
111			☆☆☆☆☆
112			☆☆☆☆☆

Book List

pg	Book Name	Author	Rating
113			☆☆☆☆☆
114			☆☆☆☆☆
115			☆☆☆☆☆
116			☆☆☆☆☆
117			☆☆☆☆☆
118			☆☆☆☆☆
119			☆☆☆☆☆
120			☆☆☆☆☆
121			☆☆☆☆☆
122			☆☆☆☆☆
123			☆☆☆☆☆
124			☆☆☆☆☆
125			☆☆☆☆☆
126			☆☆☆☆☆
127			☆☆☆☆☆
128			☆☆☆☆☆
129			☆☆☆☆☆
130			☆☆☆☆☆
131			☆☆☆☆☆
132			☆☆☆☆☆

Book Log

☆☆☆☆☆

Title: ....

Author: .... Series ☐ # ....

Start Date: .... End Date: .... DNF ☐

Fiction ☐ Genre: ....

Non-Fiction ☐ Subject: ....

Paperback ☐   Hardback ☐   eBook ☐   Audio Book ☐

Summary and Characters:

....

....

....

....

....

....

Likes/Dislikes:

....

....

....

....

....

Thoughts:

....

....

....

....

....

Shared review online somewhere ☐

Book Log ☆☆☆☆☆

Title: ....

Author: .... Series ☐ # ....

Start Date: .... End Date: .... DNF ☐

Fiction ☐ Genre: ....

Non-Fiction ☐ Subject: ....

Paperback ☐ Hardback ☐ eBook ☐ Audio Book ☐

Summary and Characters:

....

....

....

....

....

....

Likes/Dislikes:

....

....

....

....

Thoughts:

....

....

....

....

Shared review online somewhere ☐

Book Log

☆☆☆☆☆

Title: ....

Author: .... Series ☐ # ....

Start Date: .... End Date: .... DNF ☐

Fiction ☐ Genre: ....

Non-Fiction ☐ Subject: ....

Paperback ☐   Hardback ☐   eBook ☐   Audio Book ☐

Summary and Characters:

....

....

....

....

....

....

Likes/Dislikes:

....

....

....

....

....

Thoughts:

....

....

....

....

....

Shared review online somewhere ☐

Book Log

☆☆☆☆☆

Title: ....

Author: .... Series ☐ # ....

Start Date: .... End Date: .... DNF ☐

Fiction ☐ Genre: ....

Non-Fiction ☐ Subject: ....

Paperback ☐   Hardback ☐   eBook ☐   Audio Book ☐

Summary and Characters:

....

....

....

....

....

Likes/Dislikes:

....

....

....

....

Thoughts:

....

....

....

....

....

Shared review online somewhere ☐

Book Log

☆☆☆☆☆

Title: ....

Author: .... Series ☐ # ....

Start Date: .... End Date: .... DNF ☐

Fiction ☐ Genre: ....

Non-Fiction ☐ Subject: ....

Paperback ☐   Hardback ☐   eBook ☐   Audio Book ☐

Summary and Characters:

....

....

....

....

....

....

Likes/Dislikes:

....

....

....

....

....

Thoughts:

....

....

....

....

....

Shared review online somewhere ☐

Book Log

☆☆☆☆☆

Title: ....

Author: .... Series ☐ # ....

Start Date: .... End Date: .... DNF ☐

Fiction ☐ Genre: ....

Non-Fiction ☐ Subject: ....

Paperback ☐   Hardback ☐   eBook ☐   Audio Book ☐

Summary and Characters:

....

....

....

....

....

Likes/Dislikes:

....

....

....

....

Thoughts:

....

....

....

....

....

Shared review online somewhere ☐

Book Log

☆☆☆☆☆

Title: ....

Author: .... Series ☐ # ....

Start Date: .... End Date: .... DNF ☐

Fiction ☐ Genre: ....

Non-Fiction ☐ Subject: ....

Paperback ☐ Hardback ☐ eBook ☐ Audio Book ☐

Summary and Characters:

....

....

....

....

....

....

Likes/Dislikes:

....

....

....

....

....

Thoughts:

....

....

....

....

....

Shared review online somewhere ☐

Book Log

☆☆☆☆☆

Title: ....

Author: .... Series ☐ # ....

Start Date: .... End Date: .... DNF ☐

Fiction ☐ Genre: ....

Non-Fiction ☐ Subject: ....

Paperback ☐   Hardback ☐   eBook ☐   Audio Book ☐

Summary and Characters:

....

....

....

....

....

....

Likes/Dislikes:

....

....

....

....

Thoughts:

....

....

....

....

Shared review online somewhere ☐

Book Log

☆☆☆☆☆

Title: ....

Author: .... Series ☐ # ....

Start Date: .... End Date: .... DNF ☐

Fiction ☐ Genre: ....

Non-Fiction ☐ Subject: ....

Paperback ☐   Hardback ☐   eBook ☐   Audio Book ☐

Summary and Characters:

....

....

....

....

....

Likes/Dislikes:

....

....

....

....

Thoughts:

....

....

....

....

Shared review online somewhere ☐

Book Log

☆☆☆☆☆

Title: ....

Author: .... Series ☐ # ....

Start Date: .... End Date: .... DNF ☐

Fiction ☐ Genre: ....

Non-Fiction ☐ Subject: ....

Paperback ☐ Hardback ☐ eBook ☐ Audio Book ☐

Summary and Characters:

....
....
....
....
....

Likes/Dislikes:

....
....
....
....

Thoughts:

....
....
....
....
....

Shared review online somewhere ☐

Book Log ☆☆☆☆☆

Title: ....

Author: .... Series ☐ #
....

Start Date: .... End Date: .... DNF ☐

Fiction ☐ Genre: ....

Non-Fiction ☐ Subject: ....

Paperback ☐   Hardback ☐   eBook ☐   Audio Book ☐

Summary and Characters:

....
....
....
....
....
....

Likes/Dislikes:

....
....
....
....
....

Thoughts:

....
....
....
....
....

Shared review online somewhere ☐

Book Log

☆☆☆☆☆

Title: ....

Author: .... Series ☐ # ....

Start Date: .... End Date: .... DNF ☐

Fiction ☐ Genre: ....

Non-Fiction ☐ Subject: ....

Paperback ☐   Hardback ☐   eBook ☐   Audio Book ☐

Summary and Characters:

....

....

....

....

....

Likes/Dislikes:

....

....

....

....

Thoughts:

....

....

....

....

....

Shared review online somewhere ☐

Book Log

☆☆☆☆☆

Title: ....

Author: .... Series ☐ # ....

Start Date: .... End Date: .... DNF ☐

Fiction ☐ Genre: ....

Non-Fiction ☐ Subject: ....

Paperback ☐   Hardback ☐   eBook ☐   Audio Book ☐

Summary and Characters:

....
....
....
....
....
....

Likes/Dislikes:

....
....
....
....
....

Thoughts:

....
....
....
....
....

Shared review online somewhere ☐

Book Log

☆☆☆☆☆

Title: ....

Author: .... Series ☐ # ....

Start Date: .... End Date: .... DNF ☐

Fiction ☐ Genre: ....

Non-Fiction ☐ Subject: ....

Paperback ☐   Hardback ☐   eBook ☐   Audio Book ☐

Summary and Characters:

....
....
....
....
....

Likes/Dislikes:

....
....
....
....

Thoughts:

....
....
....
....
....

Shared review online somewhere ☐

Book Log

☆☆☆☆☆

Title: ....

Author: .... Series ☐ # ....

Start Date: .... End Date: .... DNF ☐

Fiction ☐ Genre: ....

Non-Fiction ☐ Subject: ....

Paperback ☐   Hardback ☐   eBook ☐   Audio Book ☐

Summary and Characters:

....

....

....

....

....

....

Likes/Dislikes:

....

....

....

....

....

Thoughts:

....

....

....

....

....

Shared review online somewhere ☐

Book Log

☆☆☆☆☆

Title: ....

Author: .... Series ☐ # ....

Start Date: .... End Date: .... DNF ☐

Fiction ☐ Genre: ....

Non-Fiction ☐ Subject: ....

Paperback ☐   Hardback ☐   eBook ☐   Audio Book ☐

Summary and Characters:

....

....

....

....

....

Likes/Dislikes:

....

....

....

....

....

Thoughts:

....

....

....

....

....

Shared review online somewhere ☐

Book Log

☆☆☆☆☆

Title: ....

Author: .... Series ☐ #

Start Date: .... End Date: .... DNF ☐

Fiction ☐   Genre: ....

Non-Fiction ☐   Subject: ....

Paperback ☐   Hardback ☐   eBook ☐   Audio Book ☐

Summary and Characters:

....

....

....

....

....

....

Likes/Dislikes:

....

....

....

....

....

Thoughts:

....

....

....

....

....

Shared review online somewhere ☐

Book Log

☆☆☆☆☆

Title: ....

Author: .... Series ☐ # ....

Start Date: .... End Date: .... DNF ☐

Fiction ☐ Genre: ....

Non-Fiction ☐ Subject: ....

Paperback ☐   Hardback ☐   eBook ☐   Audio Book ☐

Summary and Characters:

....

....

....

....

....

....

Likes/Dislikes:

....

....

....

....

Thoughts:

....

....

....

....

....

Shared review online somewhere ☐

Book Log

☆☆☆☆☆

Title: ....

Author: .... Series ☐ # ....

Start Date: .... End Date: .... DNF ☐

Fiction ☐ Genre: ....

Non-Fiction ☐ Subject: ....

Paperback ☐   Hardback ☐   eBook ☐   Audio Book ☐

Summary and Characters:

....

....

....

....

....

....

Likes/Dislikes:

....

....

....

....

....

Thoughts:

....

....

....

....

....

Shared review online somewhere ☐

Book Log

☆☆☆☆☆

Title: ....

Author: .... Series ☐ # ....

Start Date: .... End Date: .... DNF ☐

Fiction ☐ Genre: ....

Non-Fiction ☐ Subject: ....

Paperback ☐   Hardback ☐   eBook ☐   Audio Book ☐

Summary and Characters:

....

....

....

....

....

Likes/Dislikes:

....

....

....

....

Thoughts:

....

....

....

....

....

Shared review online somewhere ☐

Book Log

☆☆☆☆☆

Title: ....

Author: .... Series ☐ #...............

Start Date: .... End Date: .... DNF ☐

Fiction ☐ Genre: ....

Non-Fiction ☐ Subject: ....

Paperback ☐   Hardback ☐   eBook ☐   Audio Book ☐

Summary and Characters:

....

....

....

....

....

....

Likes/Dislikes:

....

....

....

....

....

Thoughts:

....

....

....

....

....

Shared review online somewhere ☐

Book Log

☆☆☆☆☆

Title: ....

Author: .... Series ☐ # ....

Start Date: .... End Date: .... DNF ☐

Fiction ☐ Genre: ....

Non-Fiction ☐ Subject: ....

Paperback ☐   Hardback ☐   eBook ☐   Audio Book ☐

Summary and Characters:

....

....

....

....

....

....

Likes/Dislikes:

....

....

....

....

....

Thoughts:

....

....

....

....

....

Shared review online somewhere ☐

Book Log

☆☆☆☆☆

Title: ....

Author: .... Series ☐ #
....

Start Date: .... End Date: .... DNF ☐

Fiction ☐ Genre: ....

Non-Fiction ☐ Subject: ....

Paperback ☐   Hardback ☐   eBook ☐   Audio Book ☐

Summary and Characters:

....
....
....
....
....
....

Likes/Dislikes:

....
....
....
....

Thoughts:

....
....
....
....
....

Shared review online somewhere ☐

Book Log

☆☆☆☆☆

Title: ....

Author: .... Series ☐ # ....

Start Date: .... End Date: .... DNF ☐

Fiction ☐ Genre: ....

Non-Fiction ☐ Subject: ....

Paperback ☐   Hardback ☐   eBook ☐   Audio Book ☐

Summary and Characters:

....

....

....

....

....

Likes/Dislikes:

....

....

....

....

Thoughts:

....

....

....

....

....

Shared review online somewhere ☐

Book Log

☆☆☆☆☆

Title: ....

Author: .... Series ☐ # ....

Start Date: .... End Date: .... DNF ☐

Fiction ☐ Genre: ....

Non-Fiction ☐ Subject: ....

Paperback ☐   Hardback ☐   eBook ☐   Audio Book ☐

Summary and Characters:

....

....

....

....

....

....

Likes/Dislikes:

....

....

....

....

....

Thoughts:

....

....

....

....

....

Shared review online somewhere ☐

Book Log

☆☆☆☆☆

Title: ....

Author: .... Series ☐ # ....

Start Date: .... End Date: .... DNF ☐

Fiction ☐ Genre: ....

Non-Fiction ☐ Subject: ....

Paperback ☐   Hardback ☐   eBook ☐   Audio Book ☐

Summary and Characters:

....
....
....
....
....
....

Likes/Dislikes:

....
....
....
....
....

Thoughts:

....
....
....
....
....

Shared review online somewhere ☐

Book Log ☆☆☆☆☆

Title: ....

Author: .... Series ☐ # ....

Start Date: .... End Date: .... DNF ☐

Fiction ☐ Genre: ....

Non-Fiction ☐ Subject: ....

Paperback ☐   Hardback ☐   eBook ☐   Audio Book ☐

Summary and Characters:
....
....
....
....
....
....

Likes/Dislikes:
....
....
....
....
....

Thoughts:
....
....
....
....
....

Shared review online somewhere ☐

Book Log

☆☆☆☆☆

Title: ....

Author: .... Series ☐ # ....

Start Date: .... End Date: .... DNF ☐

Fiction ☐ Genre: ....

Non-Fiction ☐ Subject: ....

Paperback ☐   Hardback ☐   eBook ☐   Audio Book ☐

Summary and Characters:

....

....

....

....

....

Likes/Dislikes:

....

....

....

....

Thoughts:

....

....

....

....

Shared review online somewhere ☐

Book Log

☆☆☆☆☆

Title: ....

Author: .... Series ☐ #

Start Date: .... End Date: .... DNF ☐

Fiction ☐ Genre: ....

Non-Fiction ☐ Subject: ....

Paperback ☐   Hardback ☐   eBook ☐   Audio Book ☐

Summary and Characters:

....

....

....

....

....

....

Likes/Dislikes:

....

....

....

....

....

Thoughts:

....

....

....

....

....

Shared review online somewhere ☐

Book Log

☆☆☆☆☆

Title: ....

Author: .... Series ☐ # ....

Start Date: .... End Date: .... DNF ☐

Fiction ☐ Genre: ....

Non-Fiction ☐ Subject: ....

Paperback ☐   Hardback ☐   eBook ☐   Audio Book ☐

Summary and Characters:

....

....

....

....

....

Likes/Dislikes:

....

....

....

....

Thoughts:

....

....

....

....

....

Shared review online somewhere ☐

Book Log

☆☆☆☆☆

Title:

Author: Series ☐ #

Start Date: End Date: DNF ☐

Fiction ☐ Genre:

Non-Fiction ☐ Subject:

Paperback ☐   Hardback ☐   eBook ☐   Audio Book ☐

Summary and Characters:

Likes/Dislikes:

Thoughts:

Shared review online somewhere ☐

Book Log

☆☆☆☆☆

Title:

Author: .... Series ☐ #

Start Date: .... End Date: .... DNF ☐

Fiction ☐ Genre:

Non-Fiction ☐ Subject:

Paperback ☐   Hardback ☐   eBook ☐   Audio Book ☐

Summary and Characters:

....

....

....

....

....

Likes/Dislikes:

....

....

....

....

Thoughts:

....

....

....

....

Shared review online somewhere ☐

Book Log

☆☆☆☆☆

Title: ....

Author: .... Series ☐ # ....

Start Date: .... End Date: .... DNF ☐

Fiction ☐ Genre: ....

Non-Fiction ☐ Subject: ....

Paperback ☐   Hardback ☐   eBook ☐   Audio Book ☐

Summary and Characters:

....

....

....

....

....

Likes/Dislikes:

....

....

....

....

Thoughts:

....

....

....

....

Shared review online somewhere ☐

Book Log

☆☆☆☆☆

Title:

Author: .... Series ☐ #

Start Date: .... End Date: .... DNF ☐

Fiction ☐ Genre:

Non-Fiction ☐ Subject:

Paperback ☐   Hardback ☐   eBook ☐   Audio Book ☐

Summary and Characters:

Likes/Dislikes:

Thoughts:

Shared review online somewhere ☐

Book Log

☆☆☆☆☆

Title: ....

Author: .... Series ☐ # ....

Start Date: .... End Date: .... DNF ☐

Fiction ☐ Genre: ....

Non-Fiction ☐ Subject: ....

Paperback ☐ Hardback ☐ eBook ☐ Audio Book ☐

Summary and Characters:

....
....
....
....
....
....

Likes/Dislikes:

....
....
....
....
....

Thoughts:

....
....
....
....
....

Shared review online somewhere ☐

Book Log

☆☆☆☆☆

Title: ....

Author: .... Series ☐ # ....

Start Date: .... End Date: .... DNF ☐

Fiction ☐ Genre: ....

Non-Fiction ☐ Subject: ....

Paperback ☐   Hardback ☐   eBook ☐   Audio Book ☐

Summary and Characters:

....

....

....

....

....

Likes/Dislikes:

....

....

....

....

Thoughts:

....

....

....

....

....

Shared review online somewhere ☐

Book Log

☆☆☆☆☆

Title: ....

Author: .... Series ☐ # ....

Start Date: .... End Date: .... DNF ☐

Fiction ☐ Genre: ....

Non-Fiction ☐ Subject: ....

Paperback ☐   Hardback ☐   eBook ☐   Audio Book ☐

Summary and Characters:

....
....
....
....
....
....

Likes/Dislikes:

....
....
....
....

Thoughts:

....
....
....
....
....

Shared review online somewhere ☐

Book Log

☆☆☆☆☆

Title:

Author: _____ Series ☐ #

Start Date: _____ End Date: _____ DNF ☐

Fiction ☐ Genre:

Non-Fiction ☐ Subject:

Paperback ☐   Hardback ☐   eBook ☐   Audio Book ☐

Summary and Characters:

_____
_____
_____
_____
_____
_____

Likes/Dislikes:

_____
_____
_____
_____

Thoughts:

_____
_____
_____
_____
_____

Shared review online somewhere ☐

Book Log

☆☆☆☆☆

Title: ....

Author: .... Series ☐ #.........

Start Date: .... End Date: .... DNF ☐

Fiction ☐ Genre: ....

Non-Fiction ☐ Subject: ....

Paperback ☐   Hardback ☐   eBook ☐   Audio Book ☐

Summary and Characters:

....

....

....

....

....

....

Likes/Dislikes:

....

....

....

....

....

Thoughts:

....

....

....

....

....

Shared review online somewhere ☐

Book Log

☆☆☆☆☆

Title:

Author: .... Series ☐ #

Start Date: .... End Date: .... DNF ☐

Fiction ☐ Genre:

Non-Fiction ☐ Subject:

Paperback ☐   Hardback ☐   eBook ☐   Audio Book ☐

Summary and Characters:

....

....

....

....

....

Likes/Dislikes:

....

....

....

....

Thoughts:

....

....

....

....

....

Shared review online somewhere ☐

Book Log

☆☆☆☆☆

Title: ....

Author: .... Series ☐ # ....

Start Date: .... End Date: .... DNF ☐

Fiction ☐ Genre: ....

Non-Fiction ☐ Subject: ....

Paperback ☐   Hardback ☐   eBook ☐   Audio Book ☐

Summary and Characters:

....

....

....

....

....

....

Likes/Dislikes:

....

....

....

....

....

Thoughts:

....

....

....

....

....

Shared review online somewhere ☐

Book Log

☆☆☆☆☆

Title: ....

Author: .... Series ☐ # ....

Start Date: .... End Date: .... DNF ☐

Fiction ☐ Genre: ....

Non-Fiction ☐ Subject: ....

Paperback ☐   Hardback ☐   eBook ☐   Audio Book ☐

Summary and Characters:

....

....

....

....

....

....

Likes/Dislikes:

....

....

....

....

....

Thoughts:

....

....

....

....

....

....

Shared review online somewhere ☐

Book Log

☆☆☆☆☆

Title: ....

Author: .... Series ☐ # ....

Start Date: .... End Date: .... DNF ☐

Fiction ☐ Genre: ....

Non-Fiction ☐ Subject: ....

Paperback ☐   Hardback ☐   eBook ☐   Audio Book ☐

Summary and Characters:

....

....

....

....

....

....

Likes/Dislikes:

....

....

....

....

....

Thoughts:

....

....

....

....

....

Shared review online somewhere ☐

Book Log

☆☆☆☆☆

Title:

Author: Series ☐ #

Start Date: End Date: DNF ☐

Fiction ☐ Genre:

Non-Fiction ☐ Subject:

Paperback ☐ Hardback ☐ eBook ☐ Audio Book ☐

Summary and Characters:

Likes/Dislikes:

Thoughts:

Shared review online somewhere ☐

Book Log

☆☆☆☆☆

Title: ....

Author: .... Series ☐ # ....

Start Date: .... End Date: .... DNF ☐

Fiction ☐ Genre: ....

Non-Fiction ☐ Subject: ....

Paperback ☐ Hardback ☐ eBook ☐ Audio Book ☐

Summary and Characters:

....

....

....

....

....

....

Likes/Dislikes:

....

....

....

....

....

Thoughts:

....

....

....

....

....

Shared review online somewhere ☐

Book Log

☆☆☆☆☆

Title: ....

Author: .... Series ☐ # ....

Start Date: .... End Date: .... DNF ☐

Fiction ☐ Genre: ....

Non-Fiction ☐ Subject: ....

Paperback ☐   Hardback ☐   eBook ☐   Audio Book ☐

Summary and Characters:

....

....

....

....

....

....

Likes/Dislikes:

....

....

....

....

Thoughts:

....

....

....

....

....

Shared review online somewhere ☐

Book Log

☆☆☆☆☆

Title:

Author: .... Series ☐ #

Start Date: .... End Date: .... DNF ☐

Fiction ☐ Genre:

Non-Fiction ☐ Subject:

Paperback ☐ Hardback ☐ eBook ☐ Audio Book ☐

Summary and Characters:

Likes/Dislikes:

Thoughts:

Shared review online somewhere ☐

Book Log

☆☆☆☆☆

Title: ....

Author: .... **Series** ☐ **#** ....

Start Date: .... **End Date:** .... **DNF** ☐

Fiction ☐ **Genre:** ....

Non-Fiction ☐ **Subject:** ....

Paperback ☐ **Hardback** ☐ **eBook** ☐ **Audio Book** ☐

Summary and Characters:

....

....

....

....

....

....

Likes/Dislikes:

....

....

....

....

....

Thoughts:

....

....

....

....

....

Shared review online somewhere ☐

Book Log ☆☆☆☆☆

Title: ....

Author: .... Series ☐ # ....

Start Date: .... End Date: .... DNF ☐

Fiction ☐ Genre: ....

Non-Fiction ☐ Subject: ....

Paperback ☐   Hardback ☐   eBook ☐   Audio Book ☐

Summary and Characters:

....
....
....
....
....
....

Likes/Dislikes:

....
....
....
....
....

Thoughts:

....
....
....
....
....

Shared review online somewhere ☐

Book Log

☆☆☆☆☆

Title: ....

Author: .... Series ☐ # ....

Start Date: .... End Date: .... DNF ☐

Fiction ☐ Genre: ....

Non-Fiction ☐ Subject: ....

Paperback ☐   Hardback ☐   eBook ☐   Audio Book ☐

Summary and Characters:

....

....

....

....

....

....

Likes/Dislikes:

....

....

....

....

....

Thoughts:

....

....

....

....

....

Shared review online somewhere ☐

Book Log ☆☆☆☆☆

Title: ....

Author: .... Series ☐ #............

Start Date: .... End Date: .... DNF ☐

Fiction ☐ Genre: ....

Non-Fiction ☐ Subject:..

Paperback ☐   Hardback ☐   eBook ☐   Audio Book ☐

Summary and Characters:

....
....
....
....
....
....

Likes/Dislikes:

....
....
....
....
....

Thoughts:

....
....
....
....
....

Shared review online somewhere ☐

Book Log

☆☆☆☆☆

Title: ....

Author: .... Series ☐ # ....

Start Date: .... End Date: .... DNF ☐

Fiction ☐ Genre: ....

Non-Fiction ☐ Subject: ....

Paperback ☐   Hardback ☐   eBook ☐   Audio Book ☐

Summary and Characters:

....

....

....

....

....

Likes/Dislikes:

....

....

....

....

Thoughts:

....

....

....

....

....

Shared review online somewhere ☐

Book Log

☆☆☆☆☆

Title: ....

Author: .... Series ☐ # ....

Start Date: .... End Date: .... DNF ☐

Fiction ☐ Genre: ....

Non-Fiction ☐ Subject: ....

Paperback ☐   Hardback ☐   eBook ☐   Audio Book ☐

Summary and Characters:

....

....

....

....

....

....

Likes/Dislikes:

....

....

....

....

....

Thoughts:

....

....

....

....

....

Shared review online somewhere ☐

Book Log ☆☆☆☆☆

Title: ....

Author: .... Series ☐ # ....

Start Date: .... End Date: .... DNF ☐

Fiction ☐ Genre: ....

Non-Fiction ☐ Subject: ....

Paperback ☐   Hardback ☐   eBook ☐   Audio Book ☐

Summary and Characters:

....
....
....
....
....
....

Likes/Dislikes:

....
....
....
....

Thoughts:

....
....
....
....
....

Shared review online somewhere ☐

Book Log

☆☆☆☆☆☆

Title: ....

Author: .... Series ☐ # ....

Start Date: .... End Date: .... DNF ☐

Fiction ☐ Genre: ....

Non-Fiction ☐ Subject: ....

Paperback ☐ Hardback ☐ eBook ☐ Audio Book ☐

Summary and Characters:

....

....

....

....

....

....

Likes/Dislikes:

....

....

....

....

....

Thoughts:

....

....

....

....

....

Shared review online somewhere ☐

Book Log

☆☆☆☆☆

Title:...

Author:.. Series ☐ #.............

Start Date:......................... End Date:..................... DNF ☐

Fiction ☐ Genre:...

Non-Fiction ☐ Subject:...

Paperback ☐   Hardback ☐   eBook ☐   Audio Book ☐

Summary and Characters:

....

....

....

....

....

....

Likes/Dislikes:

....

....

....

....

....

Thoughts:

....

....

....

....

....

Shared review online somewhere ☐

Book Log

☆☆☆☆☆

Title: ....

Author: .... Series ☐ # ....

Start Date: .... End Date: .... DNF ☐

Fiction ☐ Genre: ....

Non-Fiction ☐ Subject: ....

Paperback ☐   Hardback ☐   eBook ☐   Audio Book ☐

Summary and Characters:

....

....

....

....

....

....

Likes/Dislikes:

....

....

....

....

....

Thoughts:

....

....

....

....

....

Shared review online somewhere ☐

Book Log

☆☆☆☆☆

Title: ....

Author: .... Series ☐ #

Start Date: .... End Date: .... DNF ☐

Fiction ☐ Genre: ....

Non-Fiction ☐ Subject: ....

Paperback ☐   Hardback ☐   eBook ☐   Audio Book ☐

Summary and Characters:

....

....

....

....

....

....

Likes/Dislikes:

....

....

....

....

Thoughts:

....

....

....

....

....

Shared review online somewhere ☐

Book Log

☆☆☆☆☆

Title: ....

Author: .... Series ☐ # ....

Start Date: .... End Date: .... DNF ☐

Fiction ☐ Genre: ....

Non-Fiction ☐ Subject: ....

Paperback ☐   Hardback ☐   eBook ☐   Audio Book ☐

Summary and Characters:

....

....

....

....

....

....

Likes/Dislikes:

....

....

....

....

....

Thoughts:

....

....

....

....

....

Shared review online somewhere ☐

Book Log

☆☆☆☆☆

Title: ....

Author: .... Series ☐ # ....

Start Date: .... End Date: .... DNF ☐

Fiction ☐ Genre: ....

Non-Fiction ☐ Subject: ....

Paperback ☐   Hardback ☐   eBook ☐   Audio Book ☐

Summary and Characters:

....

....

....

....

....

....

Likes/Dislikes:

....

....

....

....

Thoughts:

....

....

....

....

....

Shared review online somewhere ☐

Book Log

☆☆☆☆☆

Title: ....

Author: .... Series ☐ # ....

Start Date: .... End Date: .... DNF ☐

Fiction ☐ Genre: ....

Non-Fiction ☐ Subject: ....

Paperback ☐   Hardback ☐   eBook ☐   Audio Book ☐

Summary and Characters:

....

....

....

....

....

....

Likes/Dislikes:

....

....

....

....

....

Thoughts:

....

....

....

....

....

Shared review online somewhere ☐

Book Log

☆☆☆☆☆

Title:

Author: .... Series ☐ #

Start Date: .... End Date: .... DNF ☐

Fiction ☐ Genre:

Non-Fiction ☐ Subject:

Paperback ☐   Hardback ☐   eBook ☐   Audio Book ☐

Summary and Characters:

Likes/Dislikes:

Thoughts:

Shared review online somewhere ☐

Book Log

☆☆☆☆☆

Title: ....

Author: .... Series ☐ # ....

Start Date: .... End Date: .... DNF ☐

Fiction ☐ Genre: ....

Non-Fiction ☐ Subject: ....

Paperback ☐   Hardback ☐   eBook ☐   Audio Book ☐

Summary and Characters:
....
....
....
....
....
....

Likes/Dislikes:
....
....
....
....
....

Thoughts:
....
....
....
....
....

Shared review online somewhere ☐

Book Log ☆☆☆☆☆

Title: ....

Author: .... Series ☐ #............

Start Date: .... End Date: .... DNF ☐

Fiction ☐ Genre: ....

Non-Fiction ☐ Subject: ....

Paperback ☐   Hardback ☐   eBook ☐   Audio Book ☐

Summary and Characters:

....

....

....

....

....

....

Likes/Dislikes:

....

....

....

....

Thoughts:

....

....

....

....

....

Shared review online somewhere ☐

Book Log

☆☆☆☆☆

Title: ....

Author: .... Series ☐ #............

Start Date: .... End Date: .... DNF ☐

Fiction ☐ Genre: ....

Non-Fiction ☐ Subject: ....

Paperback ☐   Hardback ☐   eBook ☐   Audio Book ☐

Summary and Characters:

....

....

....

....

....

....

Likes/Dislikes:

....

....

....

....

....

Thoughts:

....

....

....

....

....

Shared review online somewhere ☐

Book Log

☆☆☆☆☆

Title: ....

Author: .... Series ☐ # ....

Start Date: .... End Date: .... DNF ☐

Fiction ☐ Genre: ....

Non-Fiction ☐ Subject: ....

Paperback ☐   Hardback ☐   eBook ☐   Audio Book ☐

Summary and Characters:

....

....

....

....

....

....

Likes/Dislikes:

....

....

....

....

Thoughts:

....

....

....

....

....

Shared review online somewhere ☐

Book Log ☆☆☆☆☆

Title: ....

Author: .... Series ☐ #...........

Start Date: .... End Date: .... DNF ☐

Fiction ☐ Genre: ....

Non-Fiction ☐ Subject: ....

Paperback ☐ Hardback ☐ eBook ☐ Audio Book ☐

Summary and Characters:

....

....

....

....

....

....

Likes/Dislikes:

....

....

....

....

Thoughts:

....

....

....

....

Shared review online somewhere ☐

Book Log

☆☆☆☆☆

Title: ....

Author: .... Series ☐ # ....

Start Date: .... End Date: .... DNF ☐

Fiction ☐ Genre: ....

Non-Fiction ☐ Subject: ....

Paperback ☐ Hardback ☐ eBook ☐ Audio Book ☐

Summary and Characters:

....

....

....

....

....

....

Likes/Dislikes:

....

....

....

....

....

Thoughts:

....

....

....

....

Shared review online somewhere ☐

Book Log

☆☆☆☆☆

Title: ....

Author: .... Series ☐ # ....

Start Date: .... End Date: .... DNF ☐

Fiction ☐ Genre: ....

Non-Fiction ☐ Subject: ....

Paperback ☐   Hardback ☐   eBook ☐   Audio Book ☐

Summary and Characters:

....
....
....
....
....
....

Likes/Dislikes:

....
....
....
....
....

Thoughts:

....
....
....
....
....

Shared review online somewhere ☐

Book Log

☆☆☆☆☆

Title: ....

Author: .... Series ☐ # ....

Start Date: .... End Date: .... DNF ☐

Fiction ☐ Genre: ....

Non-Fiction ☐ Subject: ....

Paperback ☐   Hardback ☐   eBook ☐   Audio Book ☐

Summary and Characters:

....

....

....

....

....

....

Likes/Dislikes:

....

....

....

....

....

Thoughts:

....

....

....

....

....

Shared review online somewhere ☐

Book Log

☆☆☆☆☆

Title: ....

Author: .... Series ☐ # ....

Start Date: .... End Date: .... DNF ☐

Fiction ☐ Genre: ....

Non-Fiction ☐ Subject: ....

Paperback ☐   Hardback ☐   eBook ☐   Audio Book ☐

Summary and Characters:

....

....

....

....

....

....

Likes/Dislikes:

....

....

....

....

....

Thoughts:

....

....

....

....

....

Shared review online somewhere ☐

Book Log

☆☆☆☆☆

Title: ....

Author: .... Series ☐ #............

Start Date: .... End Date: .... DNF ☐

Fiction ☐ Genre: ....

Non-Fiction ☐ Subject: ....

Paperback ☐   Hardback ☐   eBook ☐   Audio Book ☐

Summary and Characters:

....

....

....

....

....

Likes/Dislikes:

....

....

....

....

Thoughts:

....

....

....

....

....

Shared review online somewhere ☐

Book Log

☆☆☆☆☆

Title: ....

Author: .... Series ☐ #.............

Start Date: .... End Date: .... DNF ☐

Fiction ☐ Genre: ....

Non-Fiction ☐ Subject: ....

Paperback ☐   Hardback ☐   eBook ☐   Audio Book ☐

Summary and Characters:

....

....

....

....

....

....

Likes/Dislikes:

....

....

....

....

Thoughts:

....

....

....

....

Shared review online somewhere ☐

Book Log

☆☆☆☆☆

Title: ....

Author: .... Series ☐ #.............

Start Date: .... End Date: .... DNF ☐

Fiction ☐ Genre: ....

Non-Fiction ☐ Subject: ....

Paperback ☐   Hardback ☐   eBook ☐   Audio Book ☐

Summary and Characters:

....

....

....

....

....

....

Likes/Dislikes:

....

....

....

....

....

Thoughts:

....

....

....

....

....

Shared review online somewhere ☐

Book Log ☆☆☆☆☆

Title: ....

Author: .... Series ☐ # ....

Start Date: .... End Date: .... DNF ☐

Fiction ☐ Genre: ....

Non-Fiction ☐ Subject: ....

Paperback ☐   Hardback ☐   eBook ☐   Audio Book ☐

Summary and Characters:
....
....
....
....
....

Likes/Dislikes:
....
....
....
....

Thoughts:
....
....
....
....

Shared review online somewhere ☐

Book Log

☆☆☆☆☆

Title: ....

Author: .... Series ☐ # ....

Start Date: .... End Date: .... DNF ☐

Fiction ☐ Genre: ....

Non-Fiction ☐ Subject: ....

Paperback ☐   Hardback ☐   eBook ☐   Audio Book ☐

Summary and Characters:

....

....

....

....

....

Likes/Dislikes:

....

....

....

....

Thoughts:

....

....

....

....

....

Shared review online somewhere ☐

Book Log

☆☆☆☆☆

Title: ....

Author: .... Series ☐ #
....

Start Date: .... End Date: .... DNF ☐

Fiction ☐ Genre: ....

Non-Fiction ☐ Subject: ....

Paperback ☐   Hardback ☐   eBook ☐   Audio Book ☐

Summary and Characters:

....

....

....

....

....

....

....

Likes/Dislikes:

....

....

....

....

....

Thoughts:

....

....

....

....

....

Shared review online somewhere ☐

Book Log

☆☆☆☆☆

Title: ....

Author: .... Series ☐ # ....

Start Date: .... End Date: .... DNF ☐

Fiction ☐ Genre: ....

Non-Fiction ☐ Subject: ....

Paperback ☐   Hardback ☐   eBook ☐   Audio Book ☐

Summary and Characters:

....

....

....

....

....

Likes/Dislikes:

....

....

....

....

Thoughts:

....

....

....

....

Shared review online somewhere ☐

Book Log

☆☆☆☆☆

Title: ....

Author: .... Series ☐ # ....

Start Date: .... End Date: .... DNF ☐

Fiction ☐ Genre: ....

Non-Fiction ☐ Subject: ....

Paperback ☐   Hardback ☐   eBook ☐   Audio Book ☐

Summary and Characters:

....

....

....

....

....

....

Likes/Dislikes:

....

....

....

....

....

Thoughts:

....

....

....

....

....

Shared review online somewhere ☐

Book Log

☆☆☆☆☆

Title:

Author: Series ☐ #

Start Date: End Date: DNF ☐

Fiction ☐ Genre:

Non-Fiction ☐ Subject:

Paperback ☐ Hardback ☐ eBook ☐ Audio Book ☐

Summary and Characters:

Likes/Dislikes:

Thoughts:

Shared review online somewhere ☐

Book Log

☆☆☆☆☆

Title: ....

Author: .... Series ☐ # ....

Start Date: .... End Date: .... DNF ☐

Fiction ☐ Genre: ....

Non-Fiction ☐ Subject: ....

Paperback ☐   Hardback ☐   eBook ☐   Audio Book ☐

Summary and Characters:
....
....
....
....
....
....

Likes/Dislikes:
....
....
....
....
....

Thoughts:
....
....
....
....
....

Shared review online somewhere ☐

Book Log

☆☆☆☆☆

Title: ....

Author: .... Series ☐ #.........

Start Date: .... End Date: .... DNF ☐

Fiction ☐ Genre: ....

Non-Fiction ☐ Subject:...

Paperback ☐   Hardback ☐   eBook ☐   Audio Book ☐

Summary and Characters:

....

....

....

....

....

....

Likes/Dislikes:

....

....

....

....

Thoughts:

....

....

....

....

....

Shared review online somewhere ☐

Book Log

☆☆☆☆☆

Title: ....

Author: .... Series ☐ # ....

Start Date: .... End Date: .... DNF ☐

Fiction ☐ Genre: ....

Non-Fiction ☐ Subject: ....

Paperback ☐   Hardback ☐   eBook ☐   Audio Book ☐

Summary and Characters:

....

....

....

....

....

....

Likes/Dislikes:

....

....

....

....

....

Thoughts:

....

....

....

....

....

Shared review online somewhere ☐

Book Log ☆☆☆☆☆

Title:

Author: .... Series ☐ #

Start Date: .... End Date: .... DNF ☐

Fiction ☐ Genre:

Non-Fiction ☐ Subject:

Paperback ☐   Hardback ☐   eBook ☐   Audio Book ☐

Summary and Characters:

Likes/Dislikes:

Thoughts:

Shared review online somewhere ☐

Book Log

☆☆☆☆☆

Title: ....

Author: .... Series ☐ # ....

Start Date: .... End Date: .... DNF ☐

Fiction ☐ Genre: ....

Non-Fiction ☐ Subject: ....

Paperback ☐   Hardback ☐   eBook ☐   Audio Book ☐

Summary and Characters:

....

....

....

....

....

Likes/Dislikes:

....

....

....

....

Thoughts:

....

....

....

....

Shared review online somewhere ☐

Book Log

☆☆☆☆☆

Title:

Author: .... Series ☐ #

Start Date: .... End Date: .... DNF ☐

Fiction ☐ Genre:

Non-Fiction ☐ Subject:

Paperback ☐   Hardback ☐   eBook ☐   Audio Book ☐

Summary and Characters:

Likes/Dislikes:

Thoughts:

Shared review online somewhere ☐

Book Log

☆☆☆☆☆

Title: ....

Author: .... Series ☐ # ....

Start Date: .... End Date: .... DNF ☐

Fiction ☐ Genre: ....

Non-Fiction ☐ Subject: ....

Paperback ☐   Hardback ☐   eBook ☐   Audio Book ☐

Summary and Characters:

....

....

....

....

....

....

Likes/Dislikes:

....

....

....

....

Thoughts:

....

....

....

....

Shared review online somewhere ☐

Book Log

☆☆☆☆☆

Title: ....

Author: .... Series ☐ # ....

Start Date: .... End Date: .... DNF ☐

Fiction ☐ Genre: ....

Non-Fiction ☐ Subject: ....

Paperback ☐   Hardback ☐   eBook ☐   Audio Book ☐

Summary and Characters:

....

....

....

....

....

....

Likes/Dislikes:

....

....

....

....

Thoughts:

....

....

....

....

....

Shared review online somewhere ☐

Book Log

☆☆☆☆☆

Title: ....

Author: .... Series ☐ # ....

Start Date: .... End Date: .... DNF ☐

Fiction ☐ Genre: ....

Non-Fiction ☐ Subject: ....

Paperback ☐ Hardback ☐ eBook ☐ Audio Book ☐

Summary and Characters:

....
....
....
....
....
....

Likes/Dislikes:

....
....
....
....
....

Thoughts:

....
....
....
....
....

Shared review online somewhere ☐

Book Log

☆☆☆☆☆

Title: ....

Author: .... Series ☐ # ....

Start Date: .... End Date: .... DNF ☐

Fiction ☐ Genre: ....

Non-Fiction ☐ Subject: ....

Paperback ☐   Hardback ☐   eBook ☐   Audio Book ☐

Summary and Characters:

....

....

....

....

....

....

Likes/Dislikes:

....

....

....

....

....

Thoughts:

....

....

....

....

....

Shared review online somewhere ☐

Book Log

☆☆☆☆☆

Title: ....

Author: .... Series ☐ # ....

Start Date: .... End Date: .... DNF ☐

Fiction ☐ Genre: ....

Non-Fiction ☐ Subject: ....

Paperback ☐   Hardback ☐   eBook ☐   Audio Book ☐

Summary and Characters:

....

....

....

....

....

....

Likes/Dislikes:

....

....

....

....

....

Thoughts:

....

....

....

....

....

Shared review online somewhere ☐

Book Log

☆☆☆☆☆

Title: ....

Author: .... Series ☐ # ....

Start Date: .... End Date: .... DNF ☐

Fiction ☐ Genre: ....

Non-Fiction ☐ Subject: ....

Paperback ☐   Hardback ☐   eBook ☐   Audio Book ☐

Summary and Characters:

....

....

....

....

....

....

Likes/Dislikes:

....

....

....

....

....

Thoughts:

....

....

....

....

....

Shared review online somewhere ☐

Book Log

☆☆☆☆☆

Title: ....

Author: .... Series ☐ # ....

Start Date: .... End Date: .... DNF ☐

Fiction ☐ Genre: ....

Non-Fiction ☐ Subject: ....

Paperback ☐   Hardback ☐   eBook ☐   Audio Book ☐

Summary and Characters:

....

....

....

....

....

....

Likes/Dislikes:

....

....

....

....

....

Thoughts:

....

....

....

....

....

Shared review online somewhere ☐

Book Log

☆☆☆☆☆

Title: ....

Author: .... Series ☐ #

Start Date: .... End Date: .... DNF ☐

Fiction ☐ Genre: ....

Non-Fiction ☐ Subject: ....

Paperback ☐   Hardback ☐   eBook ☐   Audio Book ☐

Summary and Characters:

....

....

....

....

....

Likes/Dislikes:

....

....

....

....

Thoughts:

....

....

....

....

....

Shared review online somewhere ☐

Book Log

☆☆☆☆☆

Title: ....

Author: .... Series ☐ # ....

Start Date: .... End Date: .... DNF ☐

Fiction ☐ Genre: ....

Non-Fiction ☐ Subject: ....

Paperback ☐ Hardback ☐ eBook ☐ Audio Book ☐

Summary and Characters:

....

....

....

....

....

....

Likes/Dislikes:

....

....

....

....

Thoughts:

....

....

....

....

....

Shared review online somewhere ☐

Book Log

☆☆☆☆☆

Title: ....

Author: .... Series ☐ # ....

Start Date: .... End Date: .... DNF ☐

Fiction ☐ Genre: ....

Non-Fiction ☐ Subject: ....

Paperback ☐   Hardback ☐   eBook ☐   Audio Book ☐

Summary and Characters:

....

....

....

....

....

Likes/Dislikes:

....

....

....

....

Thoughts:

....

....

....

....

....

Shared review online somewhere ☐

Book Log

☆☆☆☆☆

Title: ....

Author: .... Series ☐ # ....

Start Date: .... End Date: .... DNF ☐

Fiction ☐ Genre: ....

Non-Fiction ☐ Subject: ....

Paperback ☐   Hardback ☐   eBook ☐   Audio Book ☐

Summary and Characters:

....
....
....
....
....
....

Likes/Dislikes:

....
....
....
....
....

Thoughts:

....
....
....
....
....

Shared review online somewhere ☐

Book Log

☆☆☆☆☆

Title: ....

Author: .... Series ☐ # ....

Start Date: .... End Date: .... DNF ☐

Fiction ☐ Genre: ....

Non-Fiction ☐ Subject: ....

Paperback ☐   Hardback ☐   eBook ☐   Audio Book ☐

Summary and Characters:

....

....

....

....

....

....

Likes/Dislikes:

....

....

....

....

....

Thoughts:

....

....

....

....

....

Shared review online somewhere ☐

Book Log

☆☆☆☆☆

Title: ....

Author: .... Series ☐ # ....

Start Date: .... End Date: .... DNF ☐

Fiction ☐ Genre: ....

Non-Fiction ☐ Subject: ....

Paperback ☐   Hardback ☐   eBook ☐   Audio Book ☐

Summary and Characters:

....

....

....

....

....

Likes/Dislikes:

....

....

....

....

Thoughts:

....

....

....

....

Shared review online somewhere ☐

Book Log

☆☆☆☆☆

Title: ....

Author: .... Series ☐ # ....

Start Date: .... End Date: .... DNF ☐

Fiction ☐ Genre: ....

Non-Fiction ☐ Subject: ....

Paperback ☐   Hardback ☐   eBook ☐   Audio Book ☐

Summary and Characters:

....

....

....

....

....

Likes/Dislikes:

....

....

....

....

Thoughts:

....

....

....

....

....

Shared review online somewhere ☐

Book Log

☆☆☆☆☆

Title: ....

Author: .... Series ☐ # ....

Start Date: .... End Date: .... DNF ☐

Fiction ☐ Genre: ....

Non-Fiction ☐ Subject: ....

Paperback ☐   Hardback ☐   eBook ☐   Audio Book ☐

Summary and Characters:

....

....

....

....

....

....

Likes/Dislikes:

....

....

....

....

Thoughts:

....

....

....

....

Shared review online somewhere ☐

Book Log

☆☆☆☆☆

Title: ....

Author: .... Series ☐ # ....

Start Date: .... End Date: .... DNF ☐

Fiction ☐ Genre: ....

Non-Fiction ☐ Subject: ....

Paperback ☐   Hardback ☐   eBook ☐   Audio Book ☐

Summary and Characters:

....
....
....
....
....

Likes/Dislikes:

....
....
....
....

Thoughts:

....
....
....
....

Shared review online somewhere ☐

Book Log

☆☆☆☆☆

Title: ....

Author: .... Series ☐ # ....

Start Date: .... End Date: .... DNF ☐

Fiction ☐ Genre: ....

Non-Fiction ☐ Subject: ....

Paperback ☐   Hardback ☐   eBook ☐   Audio Book ☐

Summary and Characters:

....

....

....

....

....

....

Likes/Dislikes:

....

....

....

....

....

Thoughts:

....

....

....

....

....

Shared review online somewhere ☐

Book Log

☆☆☆☆☆

Title:	
Author:	Series ☐ #
Start Date:	End Date: DNF ☐
Fiction ☐ Genre:	
Non-Fiction ☐ Subject:	
Paperback ☐ Hardback ☐ eBook ☐ Audio Book ☐	

Summary and Characters:

....

....

....

....

....

....

Likes/Dislikes:

....

....

....

....

Thoughts:

....

....

....

....

....

Shared review online somewhere ☐

Book Log

☆☆☆☆☆

Title: ....

Author: .... Series ☐ # ....

Start Date: .... End Date: .... DNF ☐

Fiction ☐ Genre: ....

Non-Fiction ☐ Subject: ....

Paperback ☐   Hardback ☐   eBook ☐   Audio Book ☐

Summary and Characters:

....

....

....

....

....

....

Likes/Dislikes:

....

....

....

....

....

Thoughts:

....

....

....

....

....

Shared review online somewhere ☐

Book Log

☆☆☆☆☆

Title: ....

Author: .... Series ☐ #
....

Start Date: .... End Date: .... DNF ☐

Fiction ☐ Genre: ....

Non-Fiction ☐ Subject: ....

Paperback ☐   Hardback ☐   eBook ☐   Audio Book ☐

Summary and Characters:

....

....

....

....

....

....

Likes/Dislikes:

....

....

....

....

....

Thoughts:

....

....

....

....

....

Shared review online somewhere ☐

Book Log

☆☆☆☆☆

Title: ....

Author: .... Series ☐ # ....

Start Date: .... End Date: .... DNF ☐

Fiction ☐ Genre: ....

Non-Fiction ☐ Subject: ....

Paperback ☐   Hardback ☐   eBook ☐   Audio Book ☐

Summary and Characters:

....

....

....

....

....

....

Likes/Dislikes:

....

....

....

....

....

Thoughts:

....

....

....

....

....

Shared review online somewhere ☐

Book Log

☆☆☆☆☆

Title: ....

Author: .... Series ☐ # ....

Start Date: .... End Date: .... DNF ☐

Fiction ☐ Genre: ....

Non-Fiction ☐ Subject: ....

Paperback ☐   Hardback ☐   eBook ☐   Audio Book ☐

Summary and Characters:

....

....

....

....

....

Likes/Dislikes:

....

....

....

....

Thoughts:

....

....

....

....

....

Shared review online somewhere ☐

Book Log

☆☆☆☆☆

Title: ....

Author: .... Series ☐ # ....

Start Date: .... End Date: .... DNF ☐

Fiction ☐ Genre: ....

Non-Fiction ☐ Subject: ....

Paperback ☐   Hardback ☐   eBook ☐   Audio Book ☐

Summary and Characters:

....

....

....

....

....

....

Likes/Dislikes:

....

....

....

....

....

Thoughts:

....

....

....

....

....

Shared review online somewhere ☐

Book Log

☆☆☆☆☆

Title: ....

Author: .... Series ☐ # ....

Start Date: .... End Date: .... DNF ☐

Fiction ☐ Genre: ....

Non-Fiction ☐ Subject: ....

Paperback ☐   Hardback ☐   eBook ☐   Audio Book ☐

Summary and Characters:

....
....
....
....
....
....

Likes/Dislikes:

....
....
....
....
....

Thoughts:

....
....
....
....
....

Shared review online somewhere ☐

Book Log

☆☆☆☆☆

Title: ....

Author: .... Series ☐ # ....

Start Date: .... End Date: .... DNF ☐

Fiction ☐ Genre: ....

Non-Fiction ☐ Subject: ....

Paperback ☐   Hardback ☐   eBook ☐   Audio Book ☐

Summary and Characters:

....
....
....
....
....
....

Likes/Dislikes:

....
....
....
....

Thoughts:

....
....
....
....

Shared review online somewhere ☐

Book Log

☆☆☆☆☆

Title: ....

Author: .... Series ☐ #.........

Start Date: .... End Date: .... DNF ☐

Fiction ☐ Genre: ....

Non-Fiction ☐ Subject: ....

Paperback ☐ Hardback ☐ eBook ☐ Audio Book ☐

Summary and Characters:

....

....

....

....

....

Likes/Dislikes:

....

....

....

....

Thoughts:

....

....

....

....

Shared review online somewhere ☐

Book Log

☆☆☆☆☆

Title:

Author: .... Series ☐ #

Start Date: .... End Date: .... DNF ☐

Fiction ☐ Genre:

Non-Fiction ☐ Subject:

Paperback ☐   Hardback ☐   eBook ☐   Audio Book ☐

Summary and Characters:

Likes/Dislikes:

Thoughts:

Shared review online somewhere ☐

Book Log

☆☆☆☆☆

Title: ....

Author: .... Series ☐ # ....

Start Date: .... End Date: .... DNF ☐

Fiction ☐ **Genre:** ....

Non-Fiction ☐ **Subject:** ....

Paperback ☐ **Hardback** ☐ **eBook** ☐ **Audio Book** ☐

Summary and Characters:

....

....

....

....

....

Likes/Dislikes:

....

....

....

....

Thoughts:

....

....

....

....

Shared review online somewhere ☐

Book Log

☆☆☆☆☆

Title: ....

Author: .... Series ☐ # ....

Start Date: .... End Date: .... DNF ☐

Fiction ☐ Genre: ....

Non-Fiction ☐ Subject: ....

Paperback ☐ Hardback ☐ eBook ☐ Audio Book ☐

Summary and Characters:

....

....

....

....

....

....

Likes/Dislikes:

....

....

....

....

....

Thoughts:

....

....

....

....

....

Shared review online somewhere ☐

Book Log

☆☆☆☆☆

Title: ....

Author: .... Series ☐ # ....

Start Date: .... End Date: .... DNF ☐

Fiction ☐ Genre: ....

Non-Fiction ☐ Subject: ....

Paperback ☐   Hardback ☐   eBook ☐   Audio Book ☐

Summary and Characters:

....

....

....

....

....

....

Likes/Dislikes:

....

....

....

....

....

Thoughts:

....

....

....

....

....

Shared review online somewhere ☐

Book Log ☆☆☆☆☆

Title: ....

Author: .... Series ☐ # ....

Start Date: .... End Date: .... DNF ☐

Fiction ☐ Genre: ....

Non-Fiction ☐ Subject: ....

Paperback ☐   Hardback ☐   eBook ☐   Audio Book ☐

Summary and Characters:

....

....

....

....

....

Likes/Dislikes:

....

....

....

....

Thoughts:

....

....

....

....

....

Shared review online somewhere ☐

Book Log

☆☆☆☆☆

Title: ....

Author: .... **Series** ☐ **#** ....

Start Date: .... **End Date:** .... **DNF** ☐

Fiction ☐ **Genre:** ....

Non-Fiction ☐ **Subject:** ....

Paperback ☐   **Hardback** ☐   **eBook** ☐   **Audio Book** ☐

Summary and Characters:

....

....

....

....

....

Likes/Dislikes:

....

....

....

....

Thoughts:

....

....

....

....

Shared review online somewhere ☐

Book Log

☆☆☆☆☆☆

Title: ....

Author: .... Series ☐ # ....

Start Date: .... End Date: .... DNF ☐

Fiction ☐ Genre: ....

Non-Fiction ☐ Subject: ....

Paperback ☐   Hardback ☐   eBook ☐   Audio Book ☐

Summary and Characters:

....

....

....

....

....

Likes/Dislikes:

....

....

....

....

Thoughts:

....

....

....

....

Shared review online somewhere ☐

Book Log

☆☆☆☆☆

Title: ....

Author: .... Series ☐ # ....

Start Date: .... End Date: .... DNF ☐

Fiction ☐ Genre: ....

Non-Fiction ☐ Subject: ....

Paperback ☐   Hardback ☐   eBook ☐   Audio Book ☐

Summary and Characters:

....

....

....

....

....

....

Likes/Dislikes:

....

....

....

....

....

Thoughts:

....

....

....

....

....

Shared review online somewhere ☐

Favorite Reads

Favorite Characters

Name:

Book:

Why they're awesome:

Name:

Book:

Why they're awesome:

Name:

Book:

Why they're awesome:

Name:

Book:

Why they're awesome:

Name:

Book:

Why they're awesome:

Name:

Book:

Why they're awesome:

Name:

Book:

Why they're awesome:

Name:

Book:

Why they're awesome:

Name:

Book:

Why they're awesome:

Favorite Quotes

"

Book:

"

Book:

"

Book:

"

Book:

"

Book:

Favorite Quotes

"

Book:

"

Book:

"

Book:

"

Book:

"

Book:

Favorite Quotes

"

Book:

"

Book:

"

Book:

"

Book:

"

Book:

Favorite Quotes

"

....

....

Book:

"

....

....

Book:

"

....

....

Book:

"

....

....

Book:

"

....

....

Book:

Keep your own favorites here:

Keep your own favorites here:

Pattern Tracker

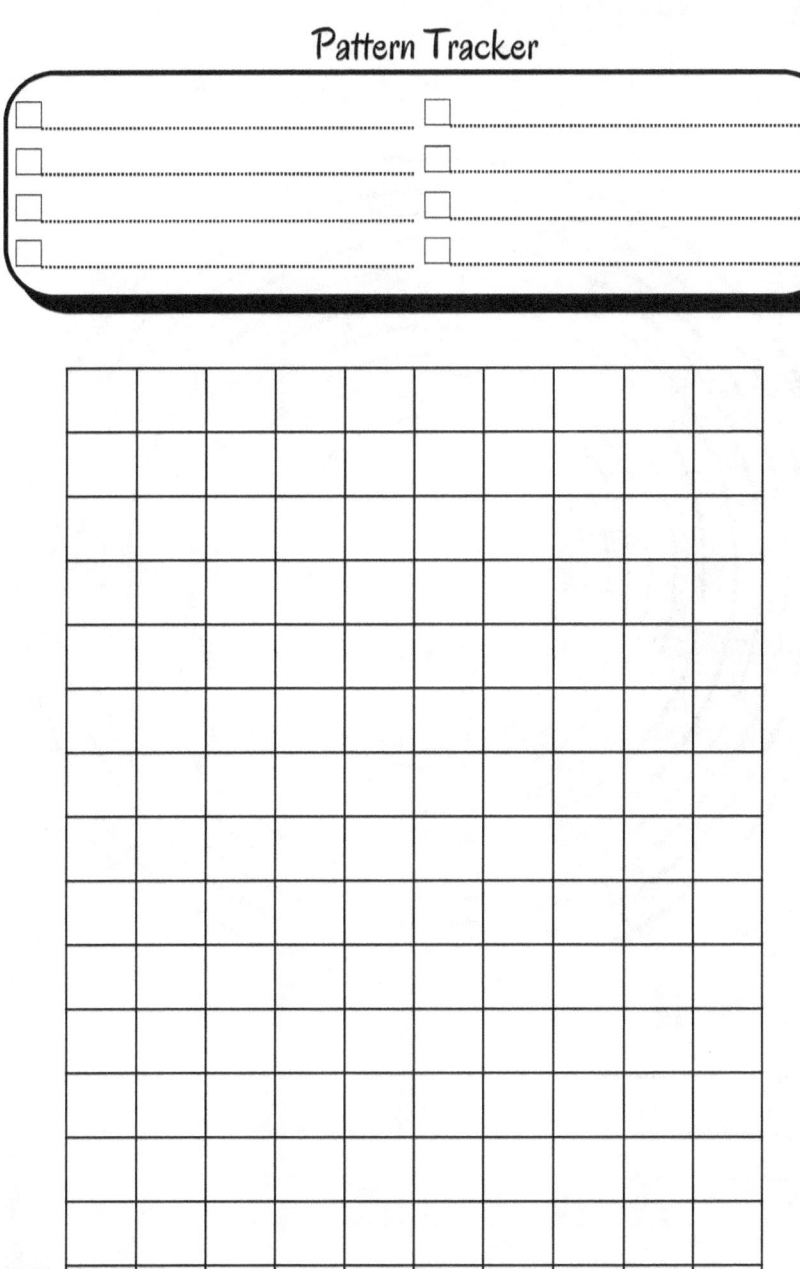

Pattern Tracker

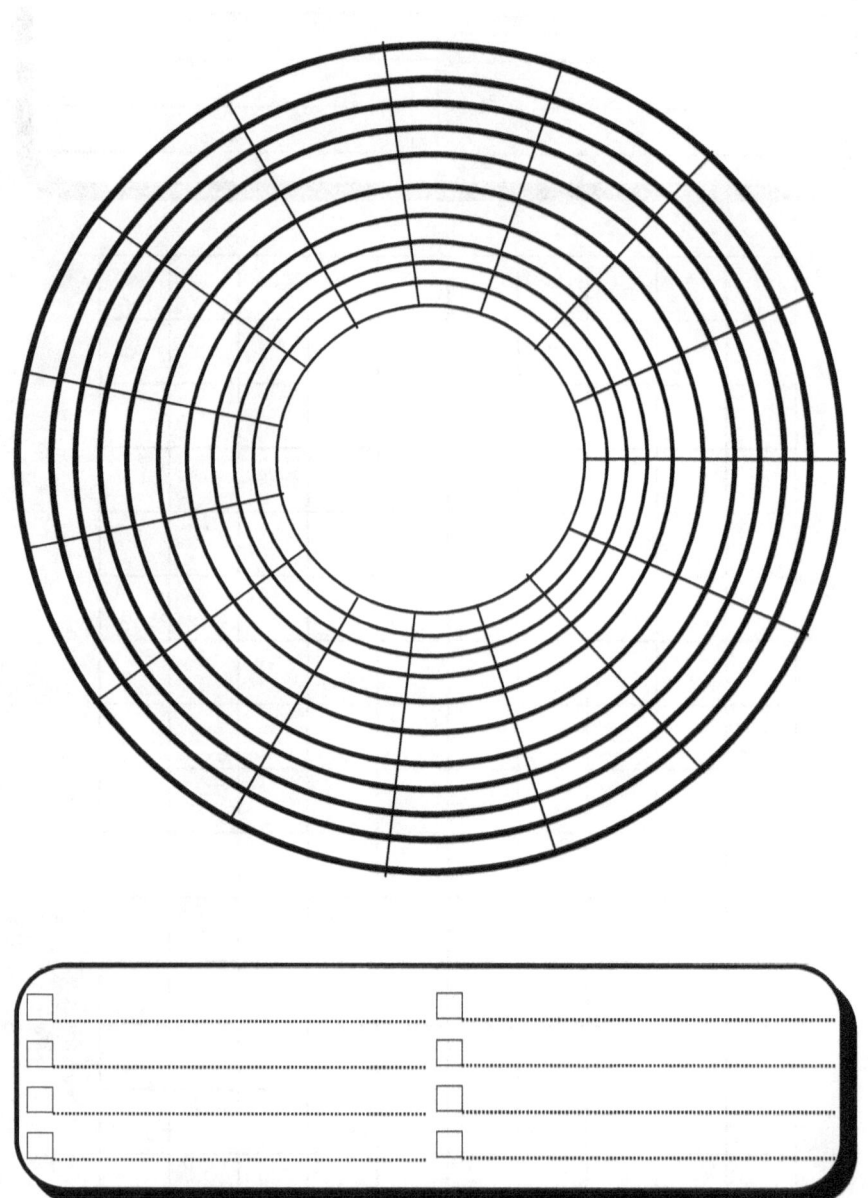

Pattern Tracker

Pattern Tracker

- [ ] ....
- [ ] ....
- [ ] ....
- [ ] ....
- [ ] ....
- [ ] ....
- [ ] ....
- [ ] ....

Reading Goals

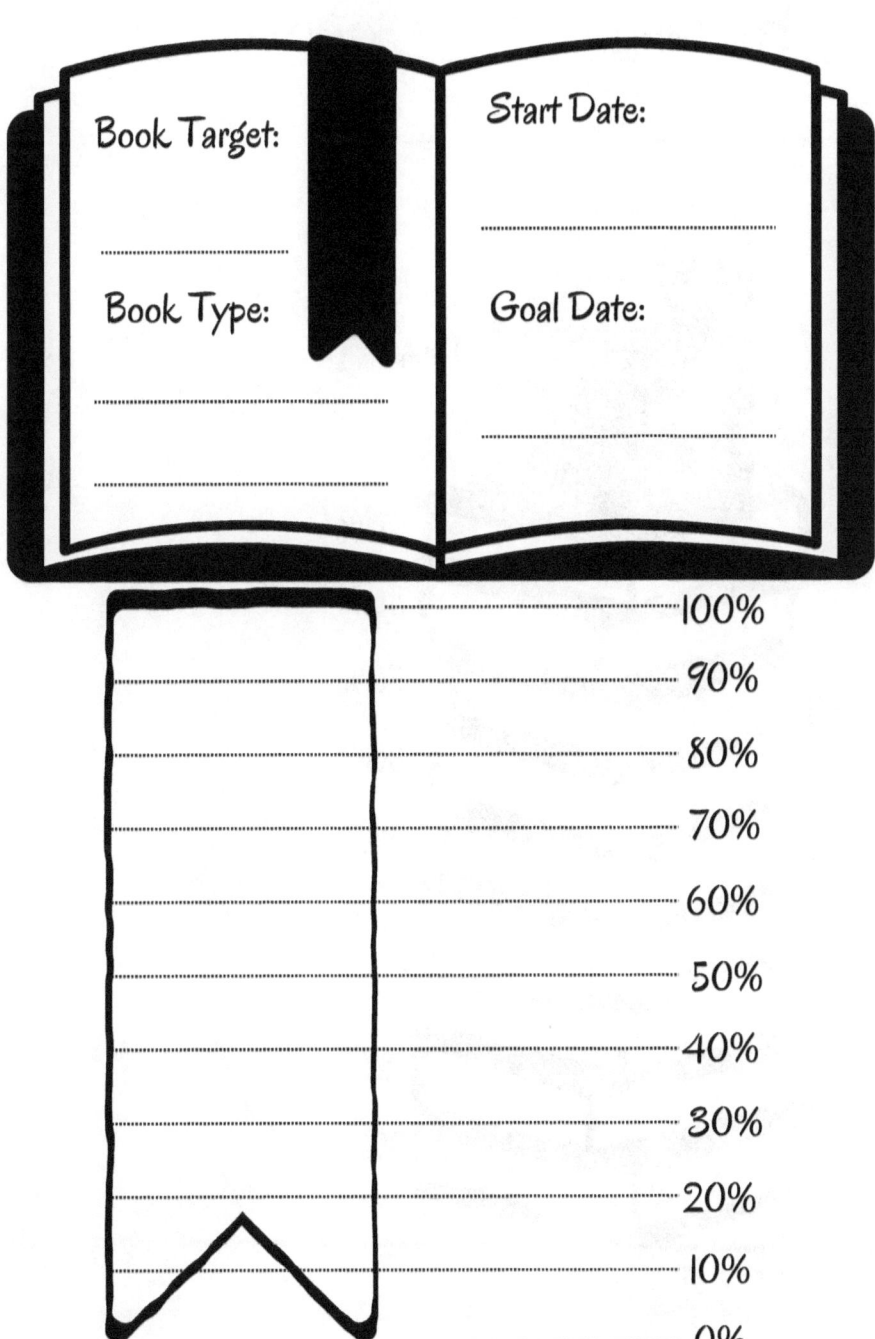

Book Target:

Book Type:

Start Date:

Goal Date:

100%
90%
80%
70%
60%
50%
40%
30%
20%
10%
0%

Reading Goals

Start Date:

Goal Date:

100%

Book Target:

90%

80%

70%

60%

50%

40%

30%

20%

10%

Reading Goals

Book Target:

Start Date:

Goal Date:

100%

90%

80%

70%

60%

50%

40%

30%

20%

10%

A Year of Reading

	January	February	March	April	May	June	July	August	September	October	November	December
1	☐	☐	☐	☐	☐	☐	☐	☐	☐	☐	☐	☐
2	☐	☐	☐	☐	☐	☐	☐	☐	☐	☐	☐	☐
3	☐	☐	☐	☐	☐	☐	☐	☐	☐	☐	☐	☐
4	☐	☐	☐	☐	☐	☐	☐	☐	☐	☐	☐	☐
5	☐	☐	☐	☐	☐	☐	☐	☐	☐	☐	☐	☐
6	☐	☐	☐	☐	☐	☐	☐	☐	☐	☐	☐	☐
7	☐	☐	☐	☐	☐	☐	☐	☐	☐	☐	☐	☐
8	☐	☐	☐	☐	☐	☐	☐	☐	☐	☐	☐	☐
9	☐	☐	☐	☐	☐	☐	☐	☐	☐	☐	☐	☐
10	☐	☐	☐	☐	☐	☐	☐	☐	☐	☐	☐	☐
11	☐	☐	☐	☐	☐	☐	☐	☐	☐	☐	☐	☐
12	☐	☐	☐	☐	☐	☐	☐	☐	☐	☐	☐	☐
13	☐	☐	☐	☐	☐	☐	☐	☐	☐	☐	☐	☐
14	☐	☐	☐	☐	☐	☐	☐	☐	☐	☐	☐	☐
15	☐	☐	☐	☐	☐	☐	☐	☐	☐	☐	☐	☐
16	☐	☐	☐	☐	☐	☐	☐	☐	☐	☐	☐	☐
17	☐	☐	☐	☐	☐	☐	☐	☐	☐	☐	☐	☐
18	☐	☐	☐	☐	☐	☐	☐	☐	☐	☐	☐	☐
19	☐	☐	☐	☐	☐	☐	☐	☐	☐	☐	☐	☐
20	☐	☐	☐	☐	☐	☐	☐	☐	☐	☐	☐	☐
21	☐	☐	☐	☐	☐	☐	☐	☐	☐	☐	☐	☐
22	☐	☐	☐	☐	☐	☐	☐	☐	☐	☐	☐	☐
23	☐	☐	☐	☐	☐	☐	☐	☐	☐	☐	☐	☐
24	☐	☐	☐	☐	☐	☐	☐	☐	☐	☐	☐	☐
25	☐	☐	☐	☐	☐	☐	☐	☐	☐	☐	☐	☐
26	☐	☐	☐	☐	☐	☐	☐	☐	☐	☐	☐	☐
27	☐	☐	☐	☐	☐	☐	☐	☐	☐	☐	☐	☐
28	☐	☐	☐	☐	☐	☐	☐	☐	☐	☐	☐	☐
29	☐	☐	☐	☐	☐	☐	☐	☐	☐	☐	☐	☐
30	☐		☐	☐	☐	☐	☐	☐	☐	☐	☐	☐
31	☐		☐		☐		☐	☐		☐		☐

To Be Read

Title: ....

Author: .... Series ☐ # ....

Owned ☐ Purchased ☐ To Buy ☐ Library Hold ☐ ARC ☐

Title: ....

Author: .... Series ☐ # ....

Owned ☐ Purchased ☐ To Buy ☐ Library Hold ☐ ARC ☐

Title: ....

Author: .... Series ☐ # ....

Owned ☐ Purchased ☐ To Buy ☐ Library Hold ☐ ARC ☐

Title: ....

Author: .... Series ☐ # ....

Owned ☐ Purchased ☐ To Buy ☐ Library Hold ☐ ARC ☐

Title: ....

Author: .... Series ☐ # ....

Owned ☐ Purchased ☐ To Buy ☐ Library Hold ☐ ARC ☐

Title: ....

Author: .... Series ☐ # ....

Owned ☐ Purchased ☐ To Buy ☐ Library Hold ☐ ARC ☐

Title: ....

Author: .... Series ☐ # ....

Owned ☐ Purchased ☐ To Buy ☐ Library Hold ☐ ARC ☐

To Be Read

Title: ....

Author: .... Series ☐ # ....

Owned☐ Purchased ☐ To Buy☐ Library Hold ☐ ARC ☐

Title: ....

Author: .... Series ☐ # ....

Owned☐ Purchased ☐ To Buy☐ Library Hold ☐ ARC ☐

Title: ....

Author: .... Series ☐ # ....

Owned☐ Purchased ☐ To Buy☐ Library Hold ☐ ARC ☐

Title: ....

Author: .... Series ☐ # ....

Owned☐ Purchased ☐ To Buy☐ Library Hold ☐ ARC ☐

Title: ....

Author: .... Series ☐ # ....

Owned☐ Purchased ☐ To Buy☐ Library Hold ☐ ARC ☐

Title: ....

Author: .... Series ☐ # ....

Owned☐ Purchased ☐ To Buy☐ Library Hold ☐ ARC ☐

Title: ....

Author: .... Series ☐ # ....

Owned☐ Purchased ☐ To Buy☐ Library Hold ☐ ARC ☐

To Be Read

Title: ....

Author: .... Series ☐ # ....

Owned☐ Purchased ☐ To Buy☐ Library Hold ☐ ARC ☐

Title: ....

Author: .... Series ☐ # ....

Owned☐ Purchased ☐ To Buy☐ Library Hold ☐ ARC ☐

Title: ....

Author: .... Series ☐ # ....

Owned☐ Purchased ☐ To Buy☐ Library Hold ☐ ARC ☐

Title: ....

Author: .... Series ☐ # ....

Owned☐ Purchased ☐ To Buy☐ Library Hold ☐ ARC ☐

Title: ....

Author: .... Series ☐ # ....

Owned☐ Purchased ☐ To Buy☐ Library Hold ☐ ARC ☐

Title: ....

Author: .... Series ☐ # ....

Owned☐ Purchased ☐ To Buy☐ Library Hold ☐ ARC ☐

Title: ....

Author: .... Series ☐ # ....

Owned☐ Purchased ☐ To Buy☐ Library Hold ☐ ARC ☐

To Be Read

Title: ....

Author: .... Series ☐ #
....

Owned☐ Purchased ☐ To Buy☐ Library Hold ☐ ARC ☐

Title: ....

Author: .... Series ☐ #
....

Owned☐ Purchased ☐ To Buy☐ Library Hold ☐ ARC ☐

Title: ....

Author: .... Series ☐ #
....

Owned☐ Purchased ☐ To Buy☐ Library Hold ☐ ARC ☐

Title: ....

Author: .... Series ☐ #
....

Owned☐ Purchased ☐ To Buy☐ Library Hold ☐ ARC ☐

Title: ....

Author: .... Series ☐ #
....

Owned☐ Purchased ☐ To Buy☐ Library Hold ☐ ARC ☐

Title: ....

Author: .... Series ☐ #
....

Owned☐ Purchased ☐ To Buy☐ Library Hold ☐ ARC ☐

Title: ....

Author: .... Series ☐ #
....

Owned☐ Purchased ☐ To Buy☐ Library Hold ☐ ARC ☐

www.ingramcontent.com/pod-product-compliance
Lightning Source LLC
Chambersburg PA
CBHW031414120626
46545CB00006B/2133